Professor Bumblebrain's Bonkers Book on... BIBLE HEROES

Copyright © Andy Robb, 2010

Published 2010 by CWR, Waverley Abbey House, Waverley Lane, Farnham, Surrey GU9 8EP, UK.
Registered Charity No. 294387. Registered Limited Company No. 1990308. Reprinted 2017.

The right of Andy Robb to be identified as the author of this work has been asserted by him in
accordance with the Copyright, Designs and Patents Act 1988.

See back of book for list of National Distributors.

Editing, design and production by CWR

Printed in Croatia by Zrinski

ISBN: 978-1-85345-578-0

Professor Bumblebrain's Bonkers Book on... BIBLE HEROES

ANDY ROBB
CWR

Welcome to my bonkers book on Bible heroes, dear reader. I am Professor Bumblebrain, and if you had been the least bit observant, you could have worked that out from the front cover of this book. If you didn't, you'll need to pull your socks up this instant! I won't tolerate sloppiness when it comes to reading one of my books. You might not have a brain the size of a large cabbage (as I do), but that is simply no excuse.

In this literary masterpiece I will be presenting to you some of the people whom I consider to be heroes (and heroines) of the Bible. You might think that you could discover them by yourself without having to empty the contents of your piggy bank to purchase this book. You *could*, but with the help of my superior intelligence you'll discover some of them much more quickly, and will, at the same time, benefit from my skilful storytelling and incisive wit.

If this book had been written for someone like me, I would have been more than happy for it to be presented as hundreds and hundreds of pages of closely typed text without even a hint of a silly cartoon to liven it up. Because you don't have anything like my brain capacity, you probably prefer information to be presented to you in a way that makes it a little easier on the eye. To that end, I have made a concession for you. How kind of me.

I am told that awards ceremonies are all the rage with young and old alike, and have therefore decided that this book will be presented to you in that particular popular format.

If the movie industry can have its Oscars then surely we can have the 'Bumblebrains' (named, obviously, after my good self, no less). I hope that this is acceptable to you all, and even if it is not you will simply have to lump it, dear reader. Let us proceed.

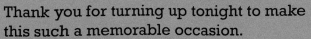

Thank you for turning up tonight to make this such a memorable occasion.
The Bible is full of people who have done heroic things, and although they might not be as brainy as me (who is?), we are nevertheless here to honour each of them with a prestigious Bumblebrain prize.

HMM, NOT A BAD LIKENESS, THOUGH I SAY IT MYSELF.

Our first award is in the category of **Gal with the Most Guts**. First, let us take a look at the life of our nominee.

This gutsy *gal* was one of Israel's leaders in the days when the nation didn't have a king. Leaders, called judges, ruled God's people and helped to keep them on track. The Israelites were being given a hard time by a guy called Jabin (a Canaanite king), and this plucky lady stepped up to the plate and decided to give the foreign fella a bloody nose. She summoned her military commander, Barak, and told him to go fight the Canaanites. Barak was a bit of a wimp and said he wouldn't go without her.

So, with Barak and 10,000 fighting men behind her, off she went to war. God threw Jabin's army into confusion and the Israelites won the day.

Next is the **Weird and Wild Award**. This goes to an exceptional chap who spent most of his life in the desert eating locusts and honey. Let us hear about the man with taste buds that you wouldn't wish on you worst enemy.

Yes, this famous fella was a relative of none other than Jesus, and was filled with the Holy Spirit before he'd even been born. He went to live in the desert and then made a bit of a name for himself by baptising people in the river Jordan and telling them that they'd better mend their wicked ways.

But this locust-eating lad wasn't interested in the fame game. He told people that God's Son (Jesus) was the one they should be keeping an eye out for.

When Jesus did eventually show up, our nominee baptised Him as well, at Jesus' request. This weird wonder of a man not only had a dodgy diet but he also wore clothes made of itchy camel hair. That'd be enough to give anyone the hump!

Our hero ended his days in the dark and dank dungeon of dastardly Herod, the local ruler, before having his head chopped off.

AN IMPORTANT HEADS UP
(sorry for the pun)

At this point you're probably thinking: Hang on a minute, didn't you say that John the Baptist had been beheaded? Well, how come he's collecting an award? If you are thinking that, it's a perfectly good thought to be having. You could even take your argument a step further and ask: For that matter, what are *any* of these Bible characters doing showing up in the twenty-first century making out as if they're still alive? Surely they all pegged it yonks ago. Well, I have to tell you that you'd be right again. Here's the point, young reader. Having these Bible heroes come back to life is purely to make this book a bit more interesting for you so that you don't die from boredom. Of course, we all know that none of them could really show up to speak for themselves.

So, here is my suggestion. Rather than trying to get your head round how long-dead Bible heroes can suddenly spring back to life and make guest appearances in this book, your best bet is to play along with my nice little game of make-believe. Don't ask too many awkward questions and everything will be just fine. Happy with that? Good. Now that's all been cleared up, it is high time we got back to the awards.

WE NOW COME TO THE CATEGORY OF BEST EXIT FROM PLANET EARTH. LET US FIND OUT WHICH BIBLE HERO IS THE WORTHY WINNER OF THIS UNUSUAL AWARD.

The nominee in this category lived at the time of wicked King Ahab of Israel and his equally nasty wife, Jezebel. The hero in question was one of God's tip-top prophets and he told it straight what God was saying.

When our main man commanded it to stop raining over the land to punish the king and queen's evil ways, it did. Just like that. Between you and me, this really didn't do much to improve things between the persistent prophet and the rogue royals. In fact, fearing for his life, he scarpered, pronto, and ended up surviving on food parcels delivered to him by ravens, followed by a widow's miraculous supply of flour and oil.

This prophet's *pièce de résistance* was when he challenged the prophets of the false god Baal to see if their god or his God could burn up a bull on an altar.

The lone prophet's God came through for him, big time, and he had the 450 prophets of Baal slaughtered. But it's because this guy went out with a bang by disappearing up to heaven in a chariot sent by God (and without the inconvenience of having to die first) that the **Best Exit from Planet Earth Award** goes to ... the prophet Elijah.

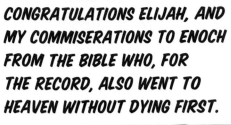

The land of Israel had been going through a bit of a bad patch and as a result the nation ended up doing the splits, so to speak. It was divided in two. The northern part of the kingdom kept the name Israel, which was handy and meant that they didn't need to change any of the road signs, while the bottom bit took the name Judah. Are you all following me so far? Excellent.

All things considered, the kings of Judah did a better job than the kings of Israel. This was helped by them holding onto Israel's capital city (Jerusalem) when they went their separate ways. This was where God's Temple was located.

The northern kingdom sort of drifted away from God quite quickly and started worshipping all manner of other odd gods. Every now and then one of the good kings would come along and do something about this. One of those good guys is the winner of our **Don't Mess with Me Award**. God proclaimed him King of Israel while a nasty guy called Joram still clung onto the job. Our man took a sneaky pot shot at Joram and killed him with a well aimed arrow.

But that wasn't the end of it. Not content with getting rid of one crooked king, he set off in hot pursuit of Judah's outgoing and equally wicked king (Ahaziah), and killed him too. To put the cherry on the cake, the winner of this award headed off to a place called Jezreel, where Queen Jezebel (Joram's mum and Ahaziah's grandma) was holed up.

The evil queen was the mastermind behind all this wickedness and the worship of idols, so she jolly well had to go as well.
As Jezebel popped her head out of an upstairs window, our hero gave the order for the queen to be thrown to the ground. Just to add insult to injury, our hero rode his chariot over Jezebel's splatted body. All I can say is that he must have had a strong stomach because the Bible tells us that he then headed off to the palace and sat down to a slap-up meal.

Interesting Info

WAY BACK IN THE DIM AND DISTANT PAST, BEFORE EVEN YOUR PARENTS WERE BORN, PEOPLE LIVED A LOT LONGER THAN THEY DO NOWADAYS.

Check out the first bit of the Bible and you'll discover that it was quite normal for someone to live to 500 years. Yes, you heard me correctly – 500 years! But I am now going to ask you to suspend your disbelief a moment longer because the winner of the next Bumblebrain wasn't satisfied with settling for a measly half a millennium (a millenium's 1,000 years, if you didn't know).

This chap didn't stop at *600* or *700* or *800* or even *900*. He chalked up a whopping *969* years on planet Earth, narrowly missing the magic number of 1,000 years by a whisker. In fact, by all accounts it seems that this long-living fellow might have even popped his clogs the very year that Noah's famous flood destroyed the world.

Are you having friends around for dinner and are tired of serving up the same old food every time? Then why not try locusts from our John the Baptist healthy eating range. Full of nutrition and very crunchy. A plate of yummy, deep-fried locusts will not only turn heads but probably stomachs as well. Buy a pack of these delicious insects today and get yourself entered into our free competition to win one of ten camelhair shirts.

DAVID

DAVID became Israel's most famous king, but along the way he made a few big boo-boos. One time he nicked the wife of a guy called Uriah and then rigged it so that the unfortunate fella got killed in battle.

King David did end up marrying the lady, Bathsheba, but their baby boy died.

Did David stay in God's bad books? Nope! OK, what he did was out of order and God told him so, but the king realised that he'd messed up big time and said sorry to God. The bottom line was that King David wanted to do right in God's eyes and that was what made him a Bible hero. In fact, God even described David as 'a man after His own heart', which means that when push came to shove, David saw things God's way and wanted to obey Him.

MARY was the sister of Martha, and they were both friends of Jesus along with their bruv, Lazarus. One time, when Jesus rocked up at their home, it seemed like Martha had ants in her pants. She fussed around and busied herself with looking after Jesus and making sure He was fed and watered.

Mary, on the other hand, simply sat at Jesus' feet and listened to what He had to say. You might think that Jesus would pick on Mary for being lazy, but you'd be wrong. He told Martha that her laid-back sister had made a good decision. Of course stuff needs to be done, but taking time out with Jesus to hear what He has to say and to learn from Him is always top of the list.

PAUL was a guy who travelled all over Europe telling people about Jesus and doing miracles to show that God was for real and that He cared about people. Paul was forever getting himself into scrapes and made a habit of getting flung into prison by people who didn't like what he had to say.

That's what happened at a place called Philippi. But did Paul and his companion Silas mope around and feel sorry for themselves? They sure didn't. Would you believe it – they actually started singing praises to God? Bible heroes like Paul don't just reserve giving credit to God for when things are going well. They do it even when things have gone pear-shaped. That's because they know that God is always good and will never dump them.

Guess what? As a result of their sing-song, God sent an earthquake to set them free. Nice one!

HANNAH

wanted kids so bad she prayed to God and said that if He gave her a son she would dedicate the lad to God to serve Him for his whole life. God heard her heartfelt prayer and, sure enough, she gave birth to a boy.

When her little lad (Samuel) was still very young, she took him to God's Temple to give the boy back to God to serve Him there. Samuel grew up to be a great prophet of God, but God gave Hannah five more kids to make things up to her. Hannah put God first, even though it cost her a lot, and that makes her a Bible hero.

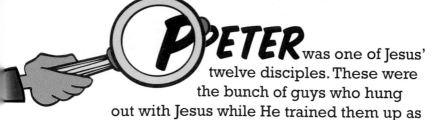

PETER was one of Jesus' twelve disciples. These were the bunch of guys who hung out with Jesus while He trained them up as His followers.

Peter was a fisherman, and when Jesus showed up and invited him on to the team, Peter downed his nets then and there, gave up his life at sea and decided to work for Jesus instead.

Let me tell you for nothing that God just loves it when we're like Peter and go for it with Him 100 per cent.

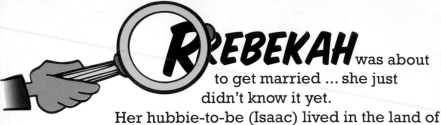

REBEKAH was about

to get married ... she just
didn't know it yet.

Her hubbie-to-be (Isaac) lived in the land of
Canaan but his dad (Abraham) wanted him to have a
wife who loved God like he did.

He sent his servant hundreds of miles away to
Mesopotamia (where his family had originally come
from) to find Isaac a bride. Abraham's servant knew that
Rebekah (a girl God led him to) was God's choice for
Isaac, but would Rebekah be
prepared to leave
her family just
because God
said so?

Well, if you hadn't
guessed already,
the answer was yes.
Rebekah was prepared
to trust God that
everything would be
OK, and that's what
makes her a Bible hero.

On with the awards. The award for the **Jammiest Bible Hero** goes to a young man who fell out with his brothers and got shipped off to Egypt to be a slave.

Because he honoured God, God blessed him and he soon became the blue-eyed boy of his Egyptian master and was put in charge of the entire household.

This cushy life came to an abrupt end when he was stitched up by the master's wife and ended up languishing in prison for years and years. While he was banged up he used his God-given ability to interpret dreams for a couple of his fellow inmates.

Years later, Egypt's Pharaoh had a couple of dreams that he was also anxious to know the meaning of, and our hero's name came into the frame.

He was quickly summoned before Pharaoh to see if he could help, and to everyone's relief he was spot on with his interpretation.

One minute this guy was locked away in a dingy dungeon and the next he was being kitted out by Pharaoh with fancy robes and promoted to Pharaoh's right hand man.

Hezekiah was a good king and he put a stop to the worship of idols throughout his nation. To his credit he also reopened and repaired God's Temple in Jerusalem – so good on you, Hezekiah! Unfortunately for this heroic king, he was struck down with a horrid sickness. In fact, Hezekiah got so ill he took to his bed and got ready to die. Hezekiah cried out to God to make him better and God came to his rescue. God's prophet Isaiah delivered the welcome news that God was going to give the king another fifteen years of life.

And what was the cure for this deadly illness? A paste made of figs. Nothing more, nothing less. Seems like a waste of perfectly good figs to me, but that's beside the point.

**So, what's so funny about this story?
I'll tell you …**

Our second potential winner in this category are husband and wife team Abraham and Sarah.
This couple crop up loads in the Bible and could win plenty of Bible hero awards between them, but here's why they are in this particular category.

God had promised Abraham that he would start a brand-new nation through his children, but Abraham and Sarah were getting on a bit – sorry to be so blunt, guys – and the chances of them having kids was about a million to one. Actually, they were probably more like a zillion to one.

It just wasn't going to happen, not at their ripe old age.

I mean, can you imagine a couple of old-timers like that showing up at the school gate with their little boy?

What a laugh!

Great-grandparents certainly, or possibly even grandparents, but mum and dad? Get away!

When Sarah first found out that God was going to give them a baby, she thought it as funny as the rest of us, and burst out laughing as well.

ANYWAY, FUNNY AS THIS STORY IS, IT WAS GOD WHO HAD THE LAST LAUGH BECAUSE THE PAST-IT PAIR DID INDEED GIVE BIRTH TO A SON, WHOM THEY CALLED ISAAC.

Ehud decided to pay the overweight king a courtesy call and pretended that he had a secret message for the tubby tyrant.

Eglon made his servants leave so that it was just him and Ehud alone in the room. Sneaky Ehud hadn't got a message for the king.

It was just a big wind-up.

What he did have, though, was a long, double-edged sword hidden under his tunic. Ehud whipped out the weapon and plunged it into King Eglon's bumper belly. The Bible handily tells us (in gory detail) how the whole sword went in, handle and all, and then Eglon's fat covered it up. Now, let's be honest, it wasn't particularly funny as far as the mega-monarch was concerned, but I'll bet even you chuckled a bit at this blubbery tale. Go on, admit it!

Some Fascinating Bible Hero Facts ...

The youngest king in the Bible was a lad called Joash. He was a good kid and obeyed God's laws and repaired God's Temple.

When King Solomon had finished building God's Temple in Jerusalem, he sacrificed to God an incredible 22,000 cattle and 120,000 sheep!

Jesus praised a Roman centurion when He showed up to heal the man's servant. Jesus said that he had more faith in God than any other Jewish person He'd ever met.

Bible hero Paul had a rough old time of it telling people about Jesus. He was shipwrecked three times, had thirty-nine lashes fives times, was beaten with rods three times and stoned once.

The prophet Elisha amazingly lived through the reign of six kings.

Gideon's mini army actually won their battle against the mahoosive Midianite army simply by surprising them in the middle of the night with trumpet blasts, the sound of breaking jars and the light from torches. The Midianites were so confused and frightened that they ended up attacking each other.

Jacob persuaded his hungry brother Esau to give him all his rights as eldest son for a measly (but yummy) bowl of stew!

Some clever person has calculated that Noah's ark could have held 125,280 sheep if they were all tightly packed together or 432 double-decker buses. Buses hadn't been invented then so Noah opted for taking animals. (My little joke.)

We now come to the Bumblebrain award for **Wimp to Warrior**, given to a man from the Bible who wasn't any great shakes in his own ability, but with God's strength did mighty things. First we'll take at the look at the life of a man called Joshua.

Joshua was one of the Israelites who'd been freed from slavery in Egypt. When God told the people of Israel that they could go and conquer the land of Canaan and make it their new home, Joshua was one of the twelve undercover agents sent in to spy out the land.

Joshua was all for going ahead and invading Canaan but most of the Israelite spies were dead against the idea. Far too risky they thought.

Because of their cowardice, the Israelites had to wait another forty fiendishly frustrating years for a second bite of the cherry, and this time round it was Joshua whom God had lined up to lead the army. Gulp! How scary was that?

Actually, to be fair to Joshua, he wasn't
really a wimp in the truest sense, in fact,
he was really quite a courageous fella.
But Joshua was also a guy who knew that
if he didn't have God's help, they'd be
well and truly defeated. How do we know
that Joshua needed a bit of a confidence
boost? Easy! The Bible says God kept
telling him to be strong and courageous.
It was with God's help that this Bible hero
not only led the Israelites into Canaan but
also they gradually conquered the place
(well, most of it), city by city, until it was
theirs to settle in.

WE'LL NOW CHECK OUT A GUY CALLED GIDEON.

Gideon's nation, Israel, kept taking a beating from the mean old Midianites. God was having none of this and so sent an angel to give Gideon some unexpected and very unwelcome news. God had chosen him to lead the Israelites to victory over Midian.

Gideon clearly thought that God had got the wrong man. As far as Gideon was concerned he was a nobody. As far as God was concerned this was precisely the sort of person he was looking for. Gideon wasn't completely convinced, but after a bit of persuasion, he accepted the assignment.

When Gideon saw the size of his army his confidence must have gone through the roof. Thirty-two thousand men were assembled ready for war.

God had other ideas though.
An army that big would take all the credit for any victory, and God intended that for Himself.
God set two tests for Gideon's fighting men, each designed to whittle down the army to the number that God wanted.

When God was finally done with Gideon's army, there were just 300 of the fighting fellas left.
With a cunning strategy from God, Gideon and his tiny army beat the Midianites hands down.

AND FINALLY,
LET US ONCE AGAIN
DROP IN ON KING
DAVID.

David wasn't always a king. His humble beginning was as a shepherd working out in the fields looking after his dad's flocks, which was tough stuff.

OK, so maybe David wasn't exactly a wimp, but then again he was hardly a hardened soldier, which makes what he did next even more incredible. Israel's number one enemy at that time was the pesky Philistines, and there was a stand-off between both armies.

The Philistines were playing their trump card, a giant of a warrior called Goliath, who was scaring the Israelite army silly with his terrifying taunts to come and take him on. But nobody dared. It seemed like stalemate until young David showed up with packed lunch for his brothers (who were in the army).

RA-RA DAVID

DAVID COULDN'T BELIEVE THAT THE ISRAELITES WERE LETTING SOMEONE LIKE THIS GOLIATH GET AWAY WITH BAITING THEM THE WAY HE WAS.

David decided that if nobody else was up for it then he'd take on the bully. Ignoring the laughs and jeers from Goliath (and from the Israelites), David stepped onto the battlefield armed with nothing more than the slingshot he used to ward off wild animals from his father's flocks and a handful of stones. Most of us know the rest of the story – of how daring David got a bullseye with a stone from the sling and knocked Goliath for six, killing him stone-dead. Literally!

The Bible, as you will have discovered, is jam-packed full of Bible heroes, which means we haven't got space to give everyone an award. Instead, here is my very own **Bumblebrain Hall of Fame**, where we big up some of the other Bible heroes who I think are deserving of a mention ...

FIRST UP, ABEL!

Abel

He was the world's fourth ever human being or, to put it another way, the second son of Adam and Eve. Got that? Abel was a shepherd and his big brother, Cain, was a farmer. They both offered sacrifices to God. Cain brought some of his harvest and Abel brought a lamb. God was pleased with Abel and his sacrifice, but not with Cain and his.

Cain was hopping mad that his younger brother had got into God's good books but that he hadn't, so he murdered Abel. That's surely taking sibling rivalry a bit too far!

Abel

Noah

When God originally made the world we live in, everything about it was good. When people started to go their own way and to do without God, the rot quickly set in. God was well miffed and decided to wipe the entire human race from the face of the earth with a flood, with the exception of a guy called Noah, who was different from the rest of them. He lived life God's way so God was going to save him (and his whole family) from the impending disaster. Just think, if it wasn't for Noah, none of us would even be around today. Cheers, Noah!

Abraham

When God first appeared to Abraham and told him
that he was going to kick-start a nation of people
dedicated to him, Abram (as he was called at that
time) could have responded by saying, 'Thanks
but no thanks, God. I don't want the job.' He didn't,
though. In obedience to God, Abram chose to leave
the comfort of his home and took his entire family to
a foreign land. Good on you, Abram!

Abraham (as he eventually became known) was a man
who trusted God to the hilt and obeyed Him, even when
God told him to sacrifice his one and only son, Isaac.
Fear not! God didn't let Abraham go through with it.
It was just a test of Abraham's faith in God.

If anyone deserves a place in this **Bible Heroes Hall
of Fame**, it has to be Abraham.

Jacob

You may ask: Why is someone like this man a Bible hero? Didn't he cheat his big brother Esau out of his inheritance as the eldest son? Yep, he sure did.

The good news is that God can change anybody, even a double-crosser like Jacob, who came to his senses and realised that living life on his own terms was the pits.

When Jacob let God take control of his life things changed ... and so did his name. From then on he was called Israel, and God promised that his descendants would one day be a great nation.

How's that for a turn around?

Jacob

Moses

There's loads to tell about Moses. He had plenty of claims to fame, but what sets him apart as a Bible hero boils down to the fact that what mattered to God mattered to Moses.

Not only did Moses lead the Israelite nation to freedom from slavery in Egypt, but he also acted as the middle-man between Israel and God.

Moses did his level best to help the Israelites get to know God and to obey Him. Moses knew God so well that he even got the nickname 'the friend of God'. How impressive would that look on Facebook? But the Bible also says that he was the most humble man on the face of the earth. And guess who wrote that claim to fame? Moses!

Let's be honest, only a truly humble man could ever say something like that!

Caleb

When Moses sent twelve spies into the land of Canaan to see what it was like (before the Israelites invaded it), all but two of them gave it the thumbs down. The ten said it was far too well fortified, and to make matters worse there were giants in the land. Caleb (one of the two), on the other hand, wasn't a scaredy cat, and thought that the Israelites should go for it. I mean, hadn't God said that the land was theirs for the taking?

If that was the case, they could expect God to help them win their battles. It was a no-brainer for Caleb. But sad to say, because most of the spies bottled it, another forty years passed before the Israelites actually went in and took the land.

Caleb was a hero because he trusted in God wholeheartedly.

Caleb

Samuel

Israel had been ruled by leaders called judges for hundreds of years, but the judges' time was coming to an end.

Very soon they'd be asking for a king, and Samuel was the chap who bridged the gap between the two. Israel had sort of gone off the rails at that point, and Samuel was the guy who got God's special nation back on track by making them destroy their idols and telling them to give their worship to God alone. With Samuel at the helm, Israel enjoyed a time of great peace before he helped the Israelites find their very first king.

Good on you, Samuel!

Jonathan

King Saul was Israel's first king and, between you and me, he didn't make a very good job of it. When God decided to line up a young guy called David to replace him, Saul was absolutely livid.
He did everything in his power to make David's life a misery and even attempted to kill his young successor.

To muddy the waters, the king's son, Jonathan, was best buddies with David. Even though Jonathan would have been his dad's rightful heir and become Israel's next king (if his dad hadn't made such a hash of things) he still remained loyal to David. Jonathan knew that David was God's choice and he was happy to go along with that. Now how's that for loyalty?

Elisha

This man stepped into the shoes (or maybe it was sandals) of Elijah and became Israel's main prophet. With God's power, Elisha did some amazing stuff such as bringing a young man back to life. Awesome! He's also famous for telling Naaman (the Syrian army commander) to take a dip seven times in the murky river Jordan to heal his nasty skin disease. It did the trick, though!

Elisha

Ezra

This brave chap plucked up the courage to ask King Artaxerxes of Babylon (where the Jewish people were in exile) to let him go back to Jerusalem to rebuild God's Temple, which was falling down. Not only did Ezra carry out his wish but he also got the people of Jerusalem back to worshipping God. Neat work, huh?

Esther

This Jewish girl became queen of Persia, and God used her to save His special people from destruction. Haman (the king's chief minister) didn't like the Jews one little bit and was scheming to have them wiped out.

Esther put her neck on the line to defend her people and the long and the short of it was that horrideous Haman was the one who ended up coming a cropper. He was hanged on the ginormous gallows that he'd erected to execute Esther's uncle.

Esther

Job

This godly guy tried to live a life that pleased God and everything seemed to be going well for him. One day all that changed, and Job (pronounced *Jobe*) lost all he had in a series of devastating disasters. Despite hitting rock bottom, Job refused to give up on God.

In time, things turned round for Job, and life was good once more – but that only happened because of his heroic trust in God.

Hosea

Israel's relationship with God was a fickle thing. One minute they said they loved Him, the next they were running off to make sacrifices to other gods. To give them a picture of how this made Him feel, God asked Hosea to marry an unfaithful woman. He remained faithful to her despite her cheating ways (which was the way it was for God and the Israelites).

Stephen

This fella was around at the time when the world's first church was just getting up and running (in Jerusalem). Not everyone loved this bunch of God-loving, miracle-working Christians, particularly some of the Jewish religious leaders.

Stephen (one of these Christians) was arrested on false charges. At his trial, brave Stephen laid into his accusers and told them a few home truths about how they'd missed the boat as far as God was concerned. It should come as no surprise to you that what saintly Stephen had to say didn't go down too well, and as a result the poor chap was stoned to death by the angry mob.

Stephen

Widow

My apologies, but we don't have a name for this particular lady. What we do know is that she was a widow (so that's what we'll call her) who showed up at Jerusalem's Temple and emptied her money bag (containing just two small coins) into the offering box. Why is she a Bible hero? Simple – because she didn't hold back anything from God. Everything she had was His, and that's just how God likes it.

Widow

Not only is it an honour to be presenting so many Bumblebrain awards, but we are also privileged to have some very special Bible heroes sitting in our audience tonight.

We took time out earlier to catch up with a few of these saintly celebrities. Let us see what they had to say to our interviewer.

Being one of his many wise men, I was obviously not too keen on this idea, so I asked God to tell me what the king had dreamt and what was the meaning of the dream. The good news is that God showed me. When I shared what I knew with Nebuchadnezzar, it was clear to everyone that I was spot on. Phew!

The upshot of the whole affair was that I got a rather nice job promotion from the king. It just shows that when you put God first you can make a difference wherever you are. Even in the palace of crazy King Nebuchadnezzar.

WHAT'S FASCINATING ABOUT YOUR STORY, RAHAB, IS THAT YOU WEREN'T ON GOD'S SIDE TO BEGIN WITH, WERE YOU?

Nope! I used to live in a place called Jericho, which made me and the people who lived there enemies of God's nation, the Israelites. When the Israelites and their leader, Joshua, turned up to invade us, we were wetting ourselves with fright. We'd heard all about how God had made a pathway through the middle of the Red Sea so that they could escape from Egypt. We were petrified that God was going to wipe us out like He had the Egyptian army.

YOU WERE A PROSTITUTE BACK THEN, WEREN'T YOU?

I was, but when two Israelite spies showed up looking for a place to hide, I decided that I was better off being on God's side. That's why I hid the spies so they didn't get caught. When Jericho was destroyed by the Israelite army, my family and I were looked after by Joshua's lot because I'd helped them get their victory. What's even more amazing is that someone with my sort of background ended up being an ancestor of Israel's King David and later of Jesus. Just shows you what coming over to God's side can do, doesn't it?

Our final guest probably needs no introduction, but I'll give him one anyway. He's the winner of last year's Bumblebrain for **Hothead of the Year**. Put your hands together for Bible strongman ... Samson.

Er, yes, hello to you as well, Samson.
Now, Samson, I know that you're a man
of few words, but can you tell me why
you let your Philistine wife Delilah
in on the secret of your God-given
superhuman strength? You must have
realised she'd immediately pass the
information on to the Philistines so that
they would know how to capture you. It
seems like a crazy thing to do, telling
her the secret that it was all down to not
having your hair cut because of a vow
your mum and dad had made to God.
Why on earth did you spill the beans?

GRUNT!
GRUNT!

Because she was cute? I see. A bit shallow wasn't it? Never mind. Moving on. The Bible also tells us about all the great victories you achieved for the Israelites. How did it make you feel, slaughtering so many of your Philistine enemies?

GRUNT! GRUNT! GRUNT!

It gave you a warm and fuzzy feeling inside? Aah, how lovely! But I'll bet you didn't feel like that after Delilah double-crossed you and handed you over to them to be tied up and tortured. What was going through your mind when you found yourself with one last chance to bring death and destruction to your Philistine enemies by pulling down the supporting pillars of their temple and killing everyone inside?

GRUNT!

Oops a daisy? Hmm, an interesting thought, Samson.

Well, thank you Samson for being so forthright and articulate. That's us out of time, so a big thank you to all our studio guests and back to you Professor.

We're almost at the end of this evening's proceedings, but this award ceremony wouldn't be complete without the Bumblebrain **Hero of Heroes Award** for the Bible hero who we think has achieved something that nobody else has.
We only have one nominee in this category and it goes to someone who could have been a big shot in everyone's eyes but instead chose to put Himself last. Let's take a look at a few of the highlights of His inspiring life.

THE BUMBLEBRAIN GAZETTE

DESERT SHOWDOWN!

Messiah Man, as we have chosen to call Him, and God's number one enemy, the devil, were pitted against each other in the dusty desert to see who would crack first. Would God's Son give in to tiredness and temptation after forty days without food and suck up to the dastardly devil or would He hold His ground? After three gruelling rounds in this battle of good versus evil, God's Son came out the winner. He's obviously one to watch out for.

The DAILY BUMBLEBRAIN

SABBATH SHAKE-UP!

Messiah Man showed up again today and really rattled some of Israel's religious leaders. Whoever heard of someone getting healed on the Jewish Sabbath? Well that's precisely what's gone and happened. A man with a manky arm got miraculously healed, and all under the noses of a bunch of religious bigots who cared more about their petty man-made rules than they did about people. I don't think that this is the last we've seen of this extraordinary guy.

SHOCK HORROR!

For three years He has criss-crossed Israel telling people of God's love and demonstrating that love by healing people and performing mighty miracles.

Today all that ended right here in Jerusalem. Messiah Man was executed by Israel's Roman rulers on a wooden cross just outside the city.

It seems that Israel's religious leaders had hatched a plot to stitch Him up and have Him wrongly accused. It's difficult to believe that we've finally seen the last of a Man who has made such a positive impact on this nation over the past three years.

Don't forget that God is always on the lookout for heroes like the ones we've heard about from the Bible. Why not take a leaf out of their book and be a hero for God yourself.

What does it take to be a hero for God? Well, take another look at some of the guys and gals in this book and see what made them special. And why not also check out a copy of the Bible when you've next got some time on your hands. See if you can find some of the Bible heroes that we've missed and work out what it was that set them apart as well.

National Distributors

UK: (and countries not listed below)
CWR, Waverley Abbey House, Waverley Lane, Farnham, Surrey GU9 8EP.
Tel: (01252) 784700 Outside UK (44) 1252 784700 Email: mail@cwr.org.uk

AUSTRALIA: KI Entertainment, Unit 21 317-321 Woodpark Road, Smithfield, New South Wales 2164, Australia
Tel: 1 800 850 777 Fax: (02) 02 9604 3699 Email: sales@kientertainment.com.au

CANADA: Parasource Marketing and Distribution, PO Box 98, 55 Woodslee Avenue, Paris, Ontario N3L 3E5.
Tel: 1800 263 2664 Email: joy.kearley@parasource.com Web: www.parasource.com

GHANA: Challenge Enterprises of Ghana, PO Box 5723, Accra. Tel: (021) 222437/223249 Fax: (021) 226227
Email: ceg@africaonline.com.gh

HONG KONG: Cross Communications Ltd, 11/F Ko's House, 577 Nathan Road, Kowloon. Tel: 2780 1188
Fax: 2770 6229 Email: cross@crosshk.com

INDIA: Crystal Communications, Plot No.83,Entrenchment Road, Seshachala Society, East Marredpally,
Secunderebad - 500026 Ph:04027737145 Email:crystal_edwj@rediffmail.com or
mailcrystalcommunications@gmail.com Web: www.crystalcommunications.co.in

KENYA: Keswick Books and Gifts Ltd, PO Box 10242 - 00400, Nairobi. Tel: (020) 2226047/312639
Email: sales.keswick@africaonline.co.ke

MALAYSIA: Salvation Publishing & Distribution Sdn Bhd, 23 Jalan SS 2/64, 47300 Petaling Jaya, Selangor.
Tel: (03) 78766411/78766797 Fax: (03) 78757066/78756360 Email: info@salvationbookcentre.com

Canaanland, No. 25 Jalan PJU 1A/41B, NZX Commercial Centre, Ara Jaya, 47301 Petaling Jaya, Selangor.
Tel: (03) 7885 0540/1/2 Fax: (03) 7885 0545 Email: info@canaanland.com.my
Web: www.canaanland.com.my

NEW ZEALAND: KI Entertainment, Unit 21 317-321 Woodpark Road, Smithfield, New South Wales 2164
Australia Tel: 0800 850 777 Fax: +612 9604 3699 Email: sales@kientertainment.com.au

NIGERIA: FBFM, Helen Baugh House, 96 St Finbarr's College Road, Akoka, Lagos. Tel: (01) 7747429/4700218/
825775/827264 Email: fbfm_1@yahoo.com

PHILIPPINES: OMF Literature Inc, 776 Boni Avenue, Mandaluyong City. Tel: (02) 531 2183 Fax: (02) 531 1960
Email: gloadlaon@omflit.com

SINGAPORE: Alby Commercial Enterprises Pte Ltd, 60 Tannery Lane #04-01, Sino Industrial Building, 347805
Tel: (65) 629 27238 Fax: (65) 629 27235 Email: marketing@alby.com.sg

SOUTH AFRICA: Life Media & Distribution, CNR Hans Schoeman & Rabie Streets, Randpark Ridge,
RANDBURG 2056 TEL: (+27)0117964157 FAX (+27)0117964017 EMAIL: maxinei@lifemedia.co.za

SRI LANKA: Christombu Publications (Pvt) Ltd, Bartleet House, 65 Braybrooke Place, Colombo 2.
Tel: (+941) 2421073/2447665 Email: christombupublications@gmail.com

USA: Parasource Marketing and Distribution, PO Box 98, 55 Woodslee Avenue, Paris, Ontario N3L 3E5, Canada
Tel: 1800 263 2664 Email: joy.kearley@parasource.com Web: www.parasource.com

CWR is a Registered Charity - Number 294387
CWR is a Limited Company registered in England - Registration Number 1990308